THE

FLINTSTONES'

WACKY

INVENTIONS

Published by Bedrock Press,
an imprint of Turner Publishing, Inc.
A Subsidiary of Turner Broadcasting System, Inc.
1050 Techwood Drive, N.W.
Atlanta, Georgia 30318

First Edition 10 9 8 7 6 5 4 3 2 1
ISBN 1-878685-65-1

Distributed by Andrews and McMeel
A Universal Press Syndicate Company
4900 Main Street
Kansas City, Missouri 64112

Written by L. Spencer Humphrey
Illustrations by Alvin S. White Studio
Edited by Elizabeth Isele
Art Direction and Design by Vickey Bolling
Assistant Art Direction by Karen White-Aguilar

Color separations, film preparation, and colorizing of line art by Graphics International, Atlanta, Georgia

Printed and bound in the United States by Bertelsmann Printing and Manufacturing Corporation, Berryville, Virginia

THE FLINTSTONES' WACKY INVENTIONS

How Things Work in the Modern Stone Age

Bedrock Press

ATLANTA

WAKE uuupPPP!

The citizens of Bedrock know all about modern technology, and couples like Fred and Wilma Flintstone live right on the cutting edge. From the moment their Bird-bell alarm clock wakes them up in the morning, until Fred puts out the saber-toothed house cat at night, the happy couple is surrounded by clever inventions. Life in the Modern Stone Age is just a stone's throw from perfect!

"Time to get up, Fred," Wilma calls, as the Bird-bell hammers out the hour. *"It's a beautiful Monday morning."*

"All right, all right, I'm getting up," grumbles Fred. *"Just don't remind me it's only Monday, will ya?"*

WAKING UP IS HARD TO DO

Sleepy Bedrockians have all kinds of interesting alarm clocks. The trick is to find one that wakes up before they do!

Once Fred is finally out of bed, the latest in grooming devices—his Porcupine hair brush and his Super Bumble Bee Buzzer safety razor—tackle the daily job of making him look his best.

"You think his hair is tough? You should try being dipped in soap and rubbed on that scratchy beard!"

◄ **1.** Fred carefully grasps his clam handle.

2. Opening the ► clam outside to catch the bee.

◄ **3.** Gotcha!

4. Buzz off ► that stubble!

"I couldn't do this without my morning coffee."

CUCKOO CLOCK ALARM

This elegant cuckoo clock alarm is designed to provide as much comfort as possible for this hard-working bird. (If it weren't for the pile of sand in his hourglass, who knows how he'd know when to get out of bed!) He may not like it, but this bird is where every Bedrock day begins!

SINGING IN THE SHOWER

Nothing can beat a steamy mammoth shower to get a person ready for a busy day of splitting rocks! Fred loves to sing along with his favorite rock "oldies" as he lathers up and gives his back a good scrub. This shower is just the beginning of a long day's work for this wet and woolly beast—big jobs for a big guy!

MAMMOTH SHOWER

"Rock around the Bowl-a-Rama tonight.
Rock, Rock, Rock till we get a strike..."

Refreshed by a snorkling good shower and Wilma's famous scrambled Pterodactyl eggs, Fred is ready to handle anything Mr. Slate and the rock quarry might throw his way.

Luckily, Wilma has the latest automatic dishwasher, so she can devote all her energy to helping Fred get out the door!

"Don't forget your lunch, Fred. It's your favorite, brontowurst on toast!" Wilma says sweetly.

"At least there will be **something** to look forward to today," mutters Fred.

KITCHEN HELPERS

"Chomp! Chomp! Chomp!"

Cooking Bedrock style is a breeze with kitchen help like the popular Stegosaurus Cuisinrock food processor and the Triceratops juicer. They update the old standbys, like the Lizard eggbeater and the Mini-dino mixer. Keep your eye on the Javasaurus. He can be found beating eggs, powering automatic can openers, as well as grinding those fresh coffee beans that help Fred face another workday.

MODERN MIXERS
These Mini-dinos really mix it up!

"Now this is a sticky job. And not a drop for me to drink!"

After Wilma loads up this little fellow with beans, he's off to the races. Producing enough coffee for a fresh pot is as easy as 1, 2, 3 for Wilma and Fred. For the Javasaurus, however, it's really a grind!

JAVASAURUS COFFEE GRINDER

"Sure, sure, Fred likes his freshly ground coffee. Says it perks him up. But look what it's doing to me!"

NICE AND..

Even though the Pterodactyl eggs have been beaten and the coffee ground and brewed, it takes the warm smell of toast to finally lure Fred into the kitchen!

Drago-toaster Operating Instructions:

1) Push start button.
2) This activates stick A.
3) Stick A is connected to stick B, pushing it down (get it so far?).
4) Stick B is connected to stick C.
5) Stick C is connected to stick D, and forces stick D to go down, which raises sticks E and F.
6) Sticks E and F are each connected to the tail pullers (and the rest is toast!).

TOASTY!

Naturally, there are a number of toasters available, but this Drago-toaster is found in more Bedrock kitchens because of its stylish design and crisp control. And it is so simple to use—most of the time!

PIG-ASAURUS

X-RAY

The inside story! This X-ray picture of the Pig-asaurus at work shows just why it is the ultimate garbage machine. Notice the extra large capacity of the Pig-asaurus's stomach and the amazing speed of its digestion. Meal after meal, day after day, this garbage-eater makes clean up a snap. Obviously, the Pig-asaurus is a creature perfectly suited to its job.

GARBAGE-ASAURUS

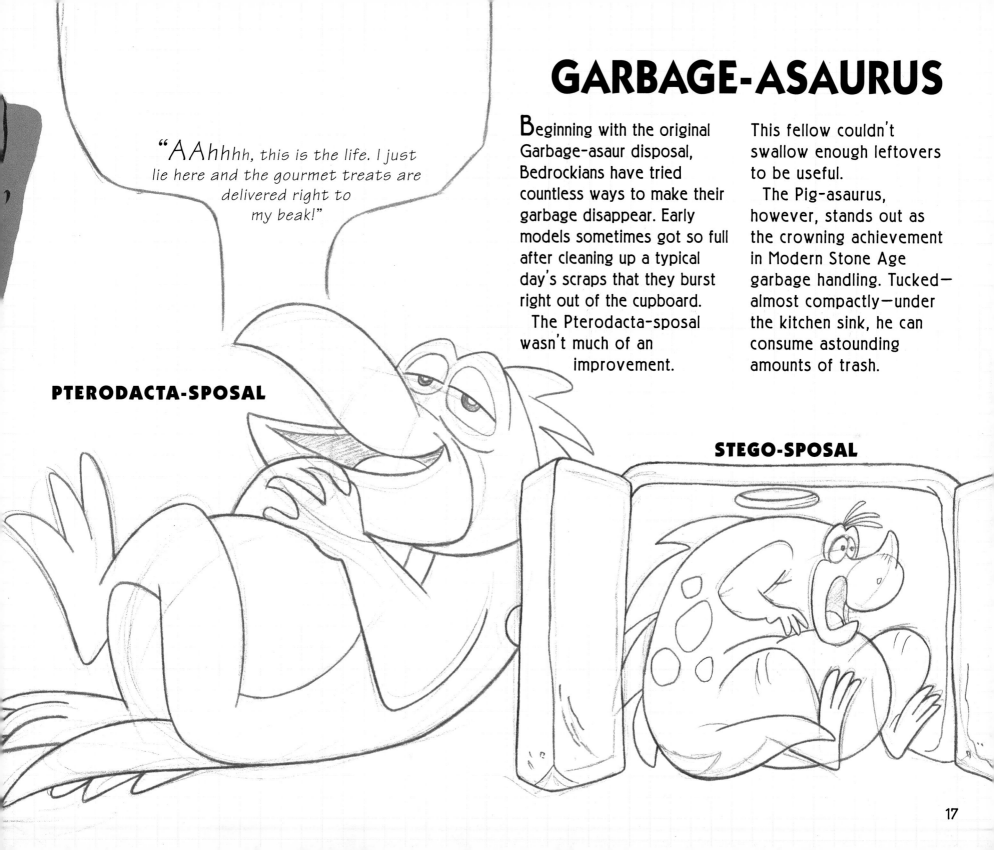

"*AAhhhh, this is the life. I just lie here and the gourmet treats are delivered right to my beak!*"

PTERODACTA-SPOSAL

Beginning with the original Garbage-asaur disposal, Bedrockians have tried countless ways to make their garbage disappear. Early models sometimes got so full after cleaning up a typical day's scraps that they burst right out of the cupboard.

The Pterodacta-sposal wasn't much of an improvement.

This fellow couldn't swallow enough leftovers to be useful.

The Pig-asaurus, however, stands out as the crowning achievement in Modern Stone Age garbage handling. Tucked—almost compactly—under the kitchen sink, he can consume astounding amounts of trash.

STEGO-SPOSAL

RUB A DUB DUB...

Wash day used to mean bending over a raging river, pounding on rocks, and hauling clean clothes back to the house. Not any more! Not with these fabulous Turb-o-matic machines.

The Pelican clothes washer handles huge loads, and even better, it walks the clothes out to the line with you!

PELICAN WASHER

"A long spin cycle can really be a pain in the neck."

WHERE'S THE GRUB!

ICE AGE BOX

MASTODON WASHER

The Flintstones used to rely on the mastodon for dish washing, until they discovered the Tortoise Combo-washer. It may be slower, but it has won their hearts by breaking fewer dishes.

GRILL

TORTOISE COMBO-WASHER

CRITTER HELPERS

Critter-powered conveniences ease household chores. But not every little mastodon qualifies for such heavy-duty work. It takes a high degree of precision, balance, and snuffability—not to mention a flexible disposition. It's a dirty job but somebody has to do it.

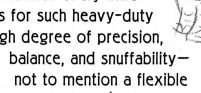

MASTO-VACUUM

Intense concentration is required to get every speck of dust and debris.

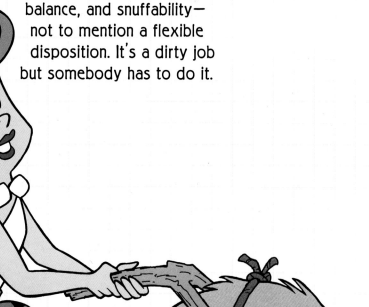

WHO'S THERE?

From the bell ringing Stegabellorus (below) to the simple but classic Bronto-knocker (right), there are doorbell styles to suit every taste. The personalized songster models are among the most popular. They include the simple push and squawk (Model A), its cousins the pull and squawk (Model C), and the tug and sing (Model D). But certainly the best-loved is the Bluebird Balanced Bell-Ringer (Model B), which is much prized for its tone and clarity.

BRONTO-KNOCKER

STEGABELLORUS

The Stegabellorus is becoming less popular these days because of his growing reputation as a lazy bum.

A.

BIRD-BELL-RINGERS

B.

C.

D.

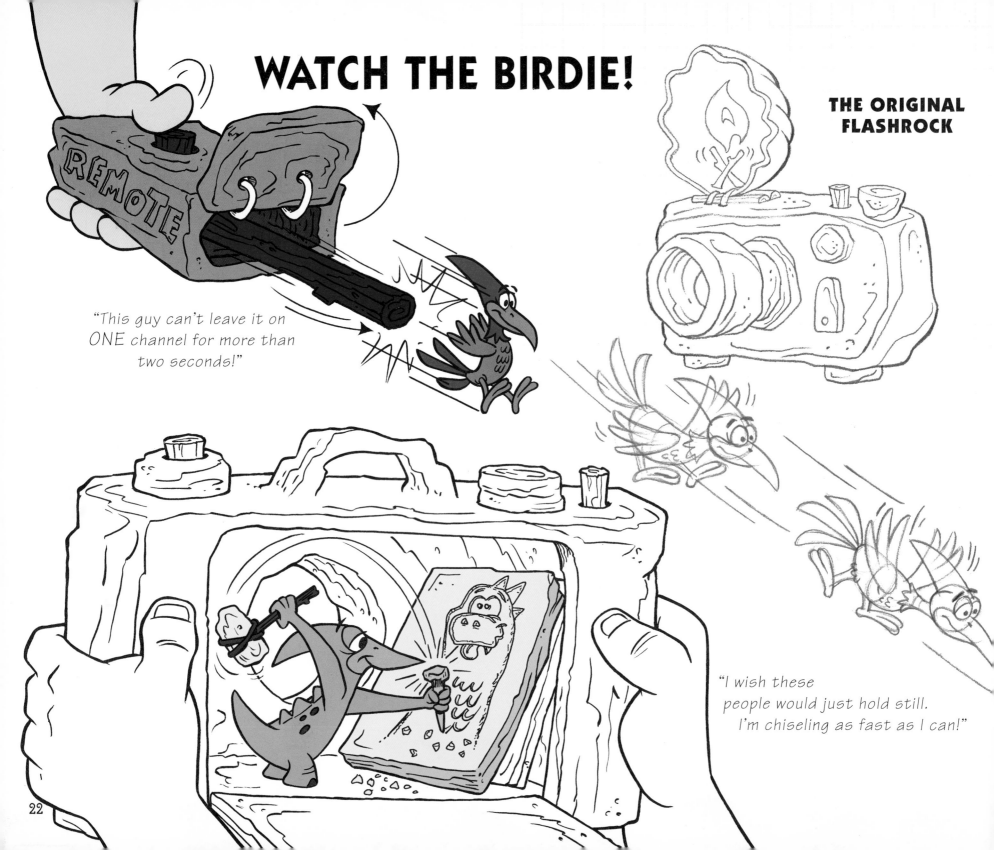

WATCH THE BIRDIE!

THE ORIGINAL FLASHROCK

"This guy can't leave it on ONE channel for more than two seconds!"

"I wish these people would just hold still. I'm chiseling as fast as I can!"

22

BIRDAROID

A brand new Birdaroid for pictures in minutes!

Wilma's got album after album of priceless slabshots taken with the Birdaroid camera.

Bedrock's cameras have certainly improved over the years. The new flash attachment helps the shutter bird take both indoor and outdoor pictures. But he still has to chisel like mad to make the "instant" picture!

The same solid, scientific thinking that produced the Modern Stone Age camera, created Fred's favorite grown-up toy—the TV remote control!

MODERN STONE AGE TV

For those homes without cable TV, Rabbit ears really improve reception.

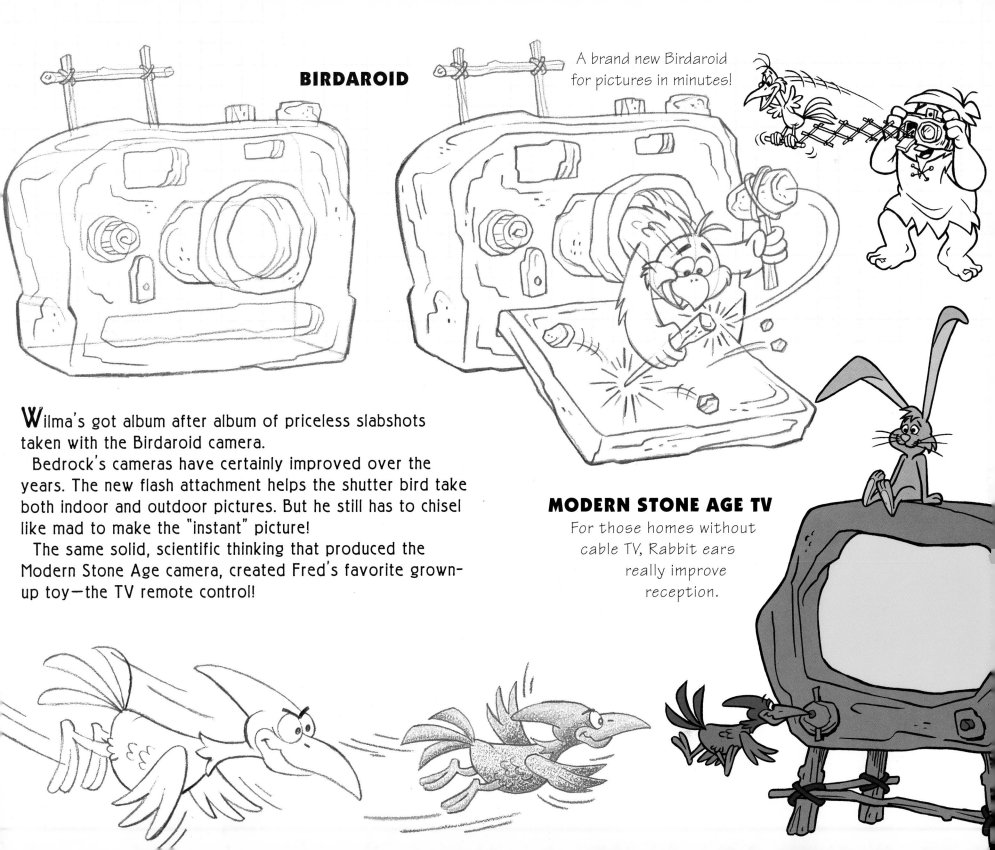

IT'S FOR YOU

Keeping in touch with friends and relatives is easy with high-tech Bedrock phones.

Early telephones included these Rock Bell models. They were reliable, but also heavy. The new Porto-tortoise models not only go where you need them, they also dial for you and tell you who's calling! That's progress!

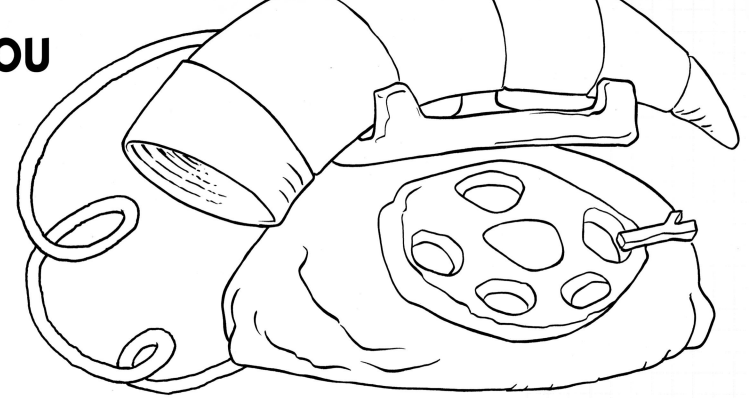

THE ORIGINAL ROCK BELL PHONE

PORTO-TORTOISE PHONE

1.

To use this early pay phone a caller simply inserted a shell and listened for the dial tone.

2.

3.

These newer models require coins to operate, but they do provide the benefit of shelter from bad weather!

"Uh-oh!
Fred is bringing Mr.
Slate home for dinner,
again!"

25

WHAT A STITCH

"It's a little dry, but at least saber-tooth hide tastes good!"

This bird takes the drudgery out of sewing for Wilma, even tough saber-tooth hides are a breeze to stitch up.

Wilma gets into gear with her sewing machine, super-sharp Pterodactyl shears, easy-to-use Snake tape measure, and pincushions by her side. She's ready for a quiet afternoon, making a new set of curtains or a party dress for Pebbles.

KNITTING MADE EASY

"Knitting is fun, especially in the spring when the Lamb-asaurus is nice and fluffy. Of course, the knitting needles need to be in the mood!"

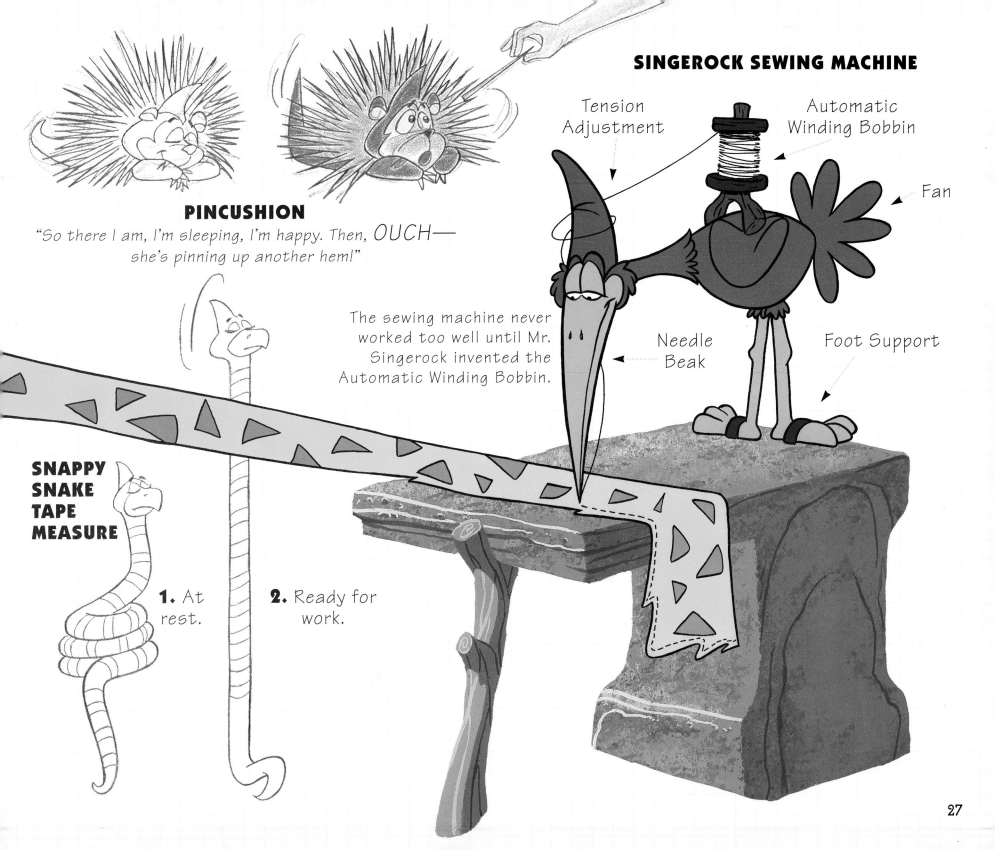

PINCUSHION

*"So there I am, I'm sleeping, I'm happy. Then, OUCH—
she's pinning up another hem!"*

SNAPPY SNAKE TAPE MEASURE

1. At rest.

2. Ready for work.

The sewing machine never worked too well until Mr. Singerock invented the Automatic Winding Bobbin.

SINGEROCK SEWING MACHINE

Tension Adjustment

Automatic Winding Bobbin

Fan

Needle Beak

Foot Support

27

TIME AFTER TIME

There are timekeepers for the home, the office, the kitchen, and even sporting events. Of course, the grandfather clock in Fred and Wilma's front hall is the envy of all their friends. But Wilma couldn't manage in the kitchen without her Monkey egg timer.

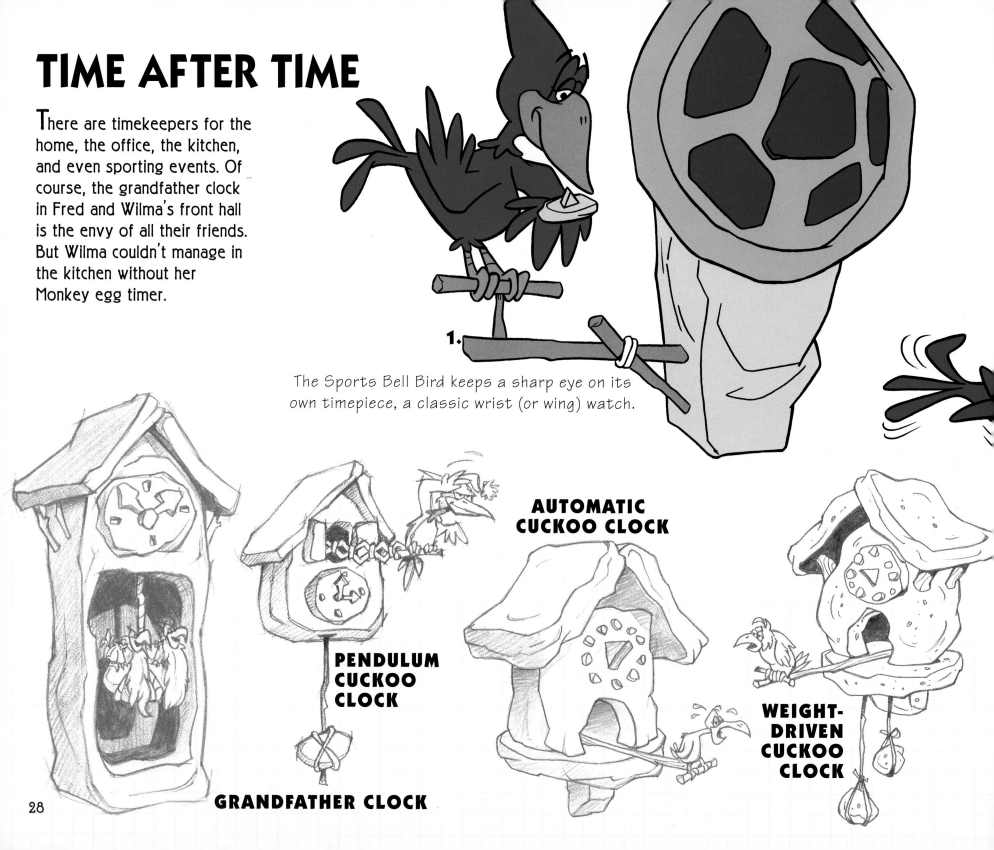

1.

The Sports Bell Bird keeps a sharp eye on its own timepiece, a classic wrist (or wing) watch.

AUTOMATIC CUCKOO CLOCK

PENDULUM CUCKOO CLOCK

WEIGHT-DRIVEN CUCKOO CLOCK

GRANDFATHER CLOCK

28

One of the most interesting timekeepers is the Sports Bell Bird. The bell has to be loud so fans at the Bedrock Gardens can hear it over their own cheers.

PRE-STONE AGE POCKET WATCH

MODERN SUNDIAL WRIST WATCH

MONKEY HOURGLASS TIMER

This fellow is found most often timing eggs and chess matches!

2.

Time's UUUUPPPPP!!! The third quarter of the game is almost over. Five. Four. Three. Two. One. BOING!!!!

3.

"Ohhhhh, what a headache I've got!"

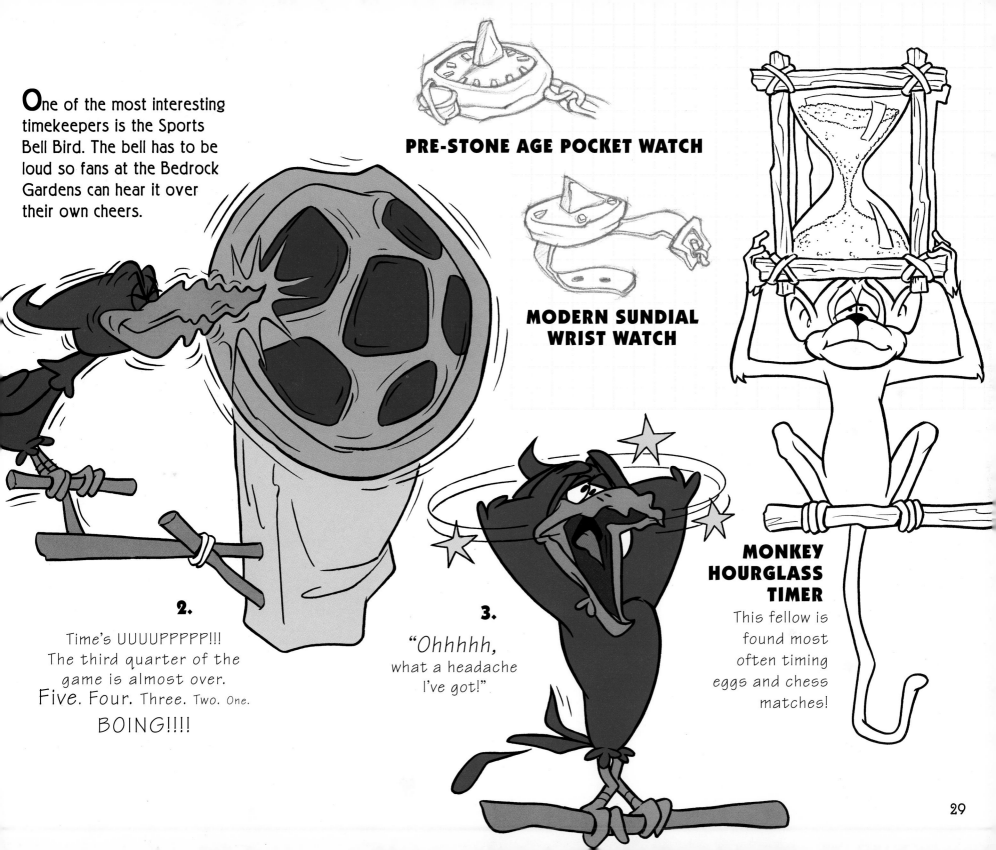

A DAY AT THE QUARRY

Rock splitting, crushing, and hauling is hard work, but Fred and the boys get a lot of help in the quarry from the heaviest modern equipment! Fred breaths a sigh of relief when the lunch whistle blows.

But just as he's about to sink his teeth into his brontowurst sandwich, Mr. Slate hollers, "**Flintstone!** *Come into [h]is office right now!*"

"**Uh-oh!** *What've I done this time?*" Fred wonders. But Mr. Slate has a big surprise for him!

HARD HAT AREA

TRICERA-DOZER

BRONTO-JACKHAMMER

TYRANNOSAURA-CRANE

Nobody works harder than the folks in the quarry—except the modern heavy equipment they use! Each and every Quarry-dino is trained for special tasks, including rock splitting, crushing, moving, hauling, and lifting—no job is too tough for these brutes.

TRICERA-TRUCK

STEGOSAURA-CRUSHER

33

TAKING CARE OF BUSINESS

From speaker phones and automatic calculators to intercoms and even that old favorite, the coffee machine, every office is loaded with Modern Stone Age equipment that helps get the job done.

The new Squawker phone is one of Bedrock's exciting pieces of office equipment. No longer are calls limited to two people. Now, Mr. Slate can put the caller "on the bird" and everyone in his office can join in the conversation.

Before the creation of the Intercom bird, Mr. Slate's secretary, Ms. Stone, used to rush in and out of his office, taking dictation and typing his letters. Thank goodness this bird was invented to speed-carry messages between the two offices, and lighten Ms. Stone's load.

Just slip a coin into the slot and this automatic Coffee-asaurus will gladly pour you a hot cup.

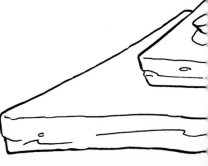

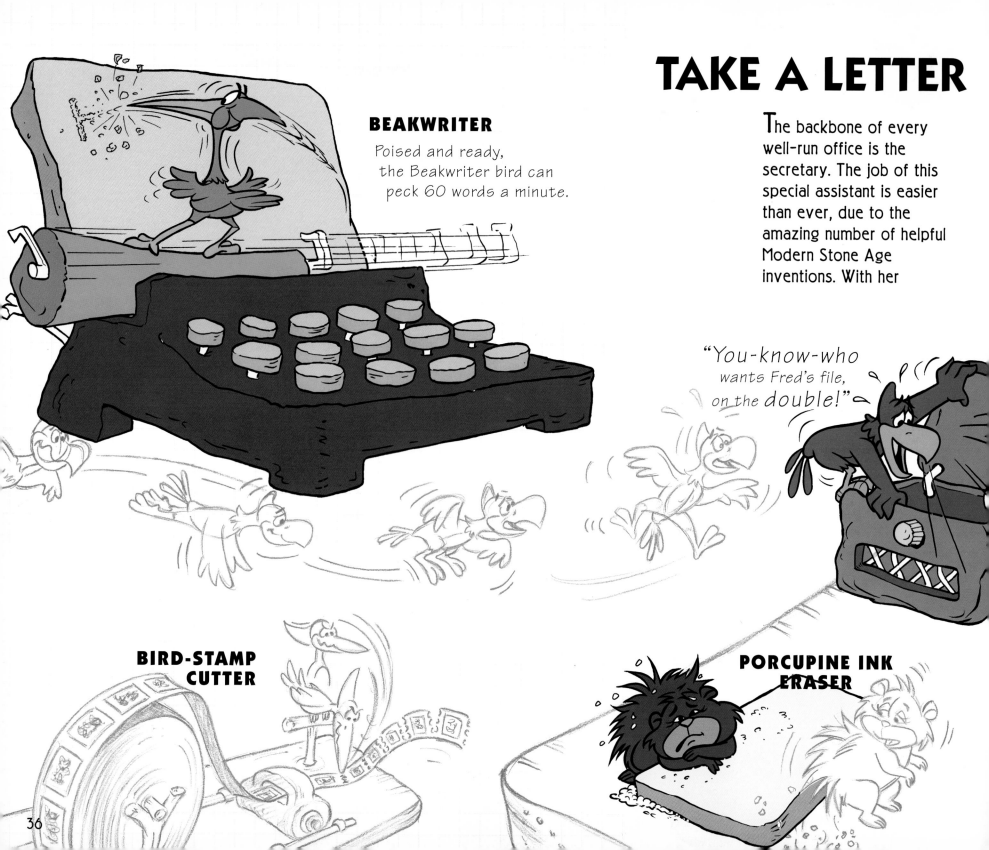

TAKE A LETTER

BEAKWRITER

Poised and ready,
the Beakwriter bird can
peck 60 words a minute.

The backbone of every well-run office is the secretary. The job of this special assistant is easier than ever, due to the amazing number of helpful Modern Stone Age inventions. With her

"You-know-who wants Fred's file, on the *double!"*

BIRD-STAMP CUTTER

PORCUPINE INK ERASER

Beakwriter, Dicta-bird, and super-quick Bird-stamp cutter, Ms. Stone keeps things in the front office humming along smoothly. And no secretary's desk is complete without a Porcupine ink eraser and a Desktop Sharpen-asaurus.

"Memo.
To Mr. Granite. From Mr. Slate.
Fifteen tons of stone have been lost somewhere
between Bedrock and Rock Vegas..."

DICTA-BIRD

DESKTOP SHARPEN-ASAURUS

COPY IT!

The office copy machine not only makes as many copies as you need, it can also reduce, enlarge, darken, or lighten your original slab.

With a simple push of a button—and thanks to these two feathered copy artists—you can get lots and lots of copies from this fabulous invention, but not without an argument!

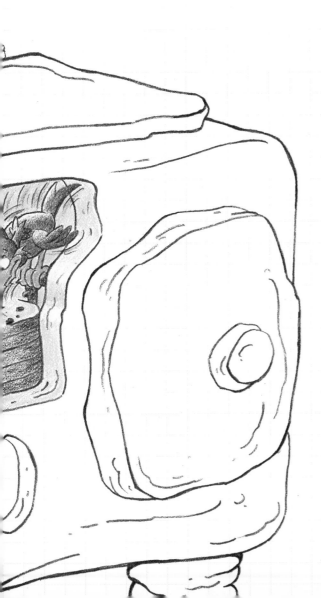

YARD WORK

After zipping through the household chores, Wilma and Betty tackle the yard work. While Betty adjusts the Mastodon nozzle to spray a fine mist for the lawn and bushes, Wilma sweeps the grass with her handy Rake-adactyl.

"I sure hope the boys take us out on the town tonight," says Wilma.

"On the town!" Betty giggles, "I can't even get Barney off the couch!"

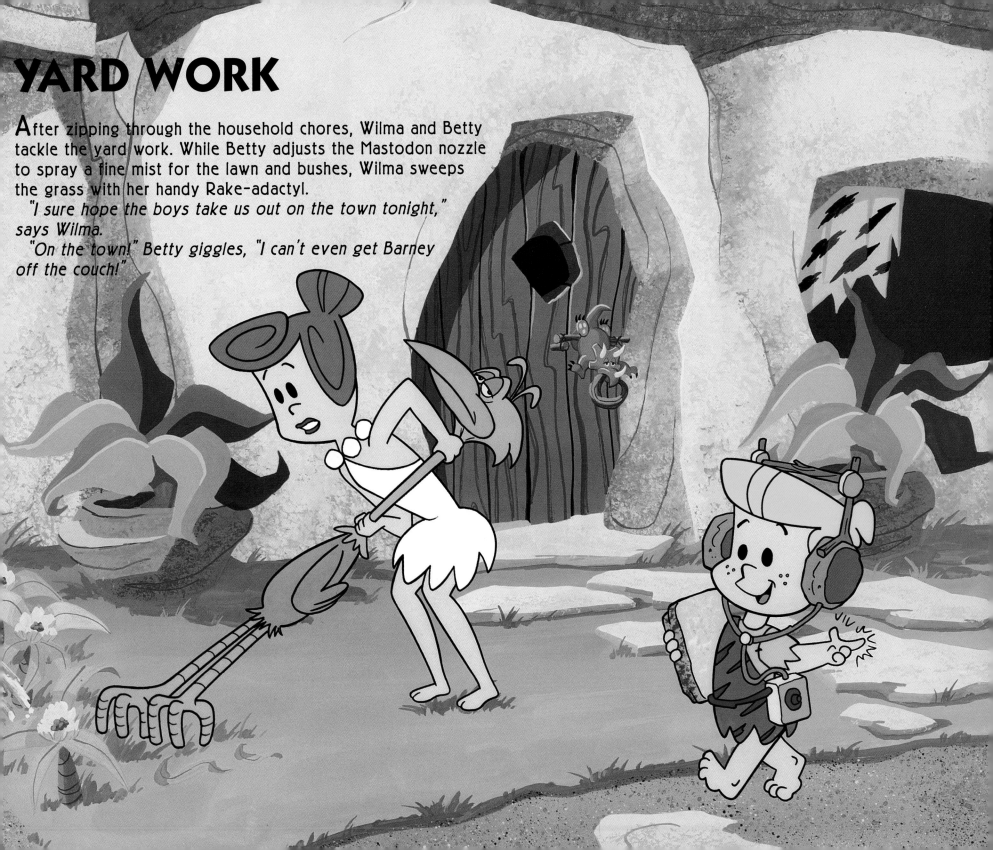

PUT IT IN THE GARAGE

To open and close the door on all this junk, Fred uses his Auto-bee garage door opener.

1) Point the Auto-bee at the closed door. Click the switch and the bee buzzes out.

2) The bee zips through the small opening in the garage door and onto the tail of the Mini-dino waiting inside.

3) The Mini-dino springs into action. It runs with all its might on a treadmill attached to the pulley system.

4) The door opens. Pretty neat!

BIRD-O-PRUNER

Fred's handy dandy Bird-o-pruner is not only a hard worker, but while cutting limbs, it keeps Fred up to date on the latest news.

TURTLE-OUTBOARD MOTOR

Fred always wanted a boat. With his new Turtle-outboard motor, he and Barney spend carefree hours puttering down Bedrock River, waiting for the fish to bite.

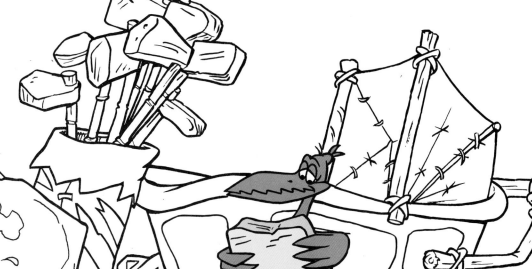

MOW THAT LAWN!

Keeping Bedrock lawns looking neat and tidy is no easy task. Barney's Dino-mower—one of the hungriest models on the market—can chomp through his half acre in almost no time at all. But it refuses to eat crabgrass, and even the smallest pebble can bring its powerful jaws to a grinding halt.

For tending her famous flower garden, Wilma is lost without her Rake-adactyl. Unfortunately, this model not only has a mind of its own, it also has tender feet!

RAKE-ADACTYL

"Oh, my aching feet!"

DINO-MOWER

BEAVER CHAINSAW

Keeping warm and cozy fires burning in Bedrock homes takes lots of wood. Thank goodness Fred's Beaver chainsaw cuts through logs in a jiffy. Fred simply pulls a ring on the beaver's collar which **(A)** sets the collar to spinning and **(B)** moves the cutting-edge saw-teeth into the log to make chunks of wood!

A.

B.

CRAB-O-MOWER

LOBST-O-MOWER

45

ROCK-AND-ROLL...

No little Bedrockians leave the house without a Bird-boom-box or Bird-headphones! Always tuned to B-ROK Radio, 77.7 on the dial, kids can listen to their favorite groups—the Sledgehammers, Saber and the Teeth, and the ever popular Rollin' Boulders.

IS HERE TO STAY!

Of course, parents may worry about the damage this high-powered rock-and-roll inflicts on young ears, but kids can't get enough of their favorites.

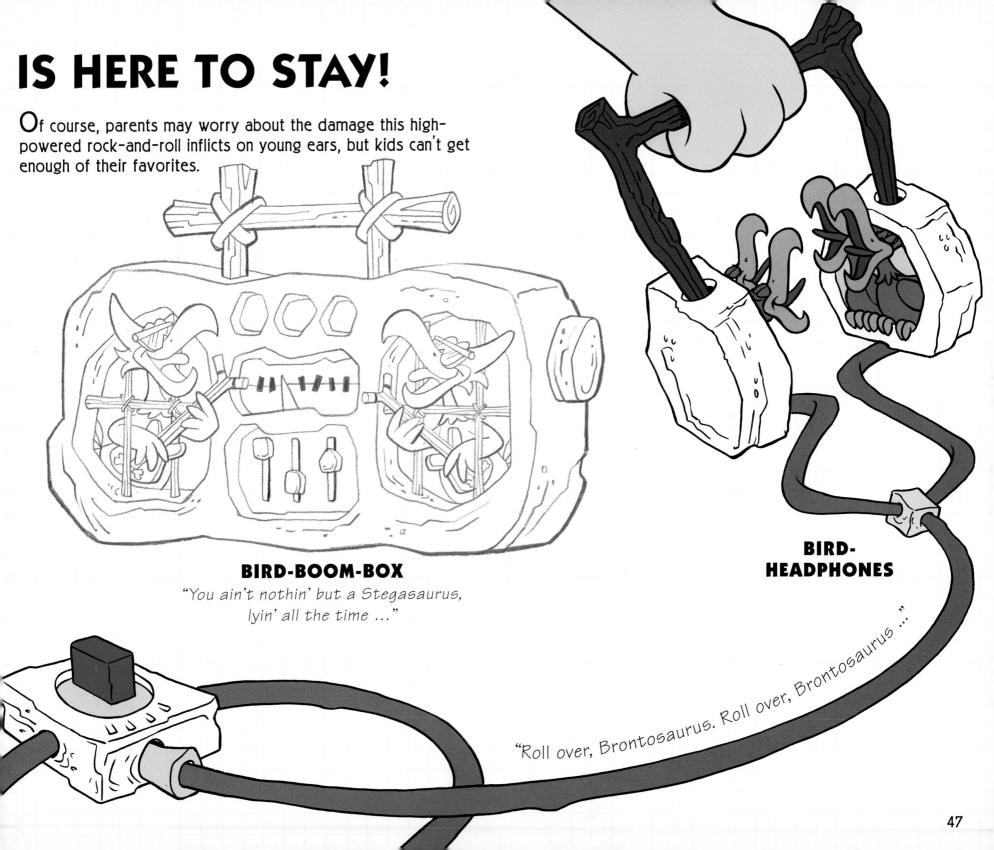

BIRD-BOOM-BOX

"You ain't nothin' but a Stegasaurus,
lyin' all the time ..."

BIRD-HEADPHONES

"Roll over, Brontosaurus. Roll over, Brontosaurus ..."

DIRECT FROM HOLLYROCK IT'S...

Just as Fred starts to tell Wilma about Mr. Slate's free passes to Bedrock Bowl-a-Rama, the phone rings.

PEBBLES AND BAMM-BAMM!

Since the kids got married and moved to glamorous Hollyrock, their parents are always happy to hear their voices. But this time, Pebbles and Bamm-Bamm have a special treat for the folks back home.

Pebbles holds the phone so it can pick up the sweet sounds of Stone Age baby talk! *"Oogi, Yabba-Dabba-Doo."* Just like Grandpa Fred! Pebbles and Bamm-Bamm live in a little Hollyrock bungalow, complete with a cozy, high-tech nursery. A darling baby dinosaur lamp casts a warm light over precious prehistoric stuffed toys. And who needs a live-in baby-sitter when you have a the Kiddie Squawk safety intercom?

ROCK-A-BYE BABY

The Modern Stone Age nursery is packed with everything busy parents need to make life with baby a joy. The Kiddie Squawk safety intercom makes sure each and every noise from the crib is heard throughout the house.

For walks to the park and drives to the shopping mall, Bedrock babies travel stylishly in comfy strollers, carriages, and car seats.

"Round and round and round I go, when babies fall asleep nobody knows!"

KIDDIE SQUAWK SAFETY INTERCOM

"Squaaaawk . . . nothing to report here. All quiet. Squaaaawk."

ANTIQUE STROLLER

CAR SAFETY SEAT

MOMMY'S SPECIAL NURSERY ROCKER

52

FUN-CAR STROLLER

TORTOISE CARRIAGE

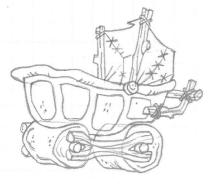

HANDI-HIGHCHAIR

AUTOMATIC DINO-SWING

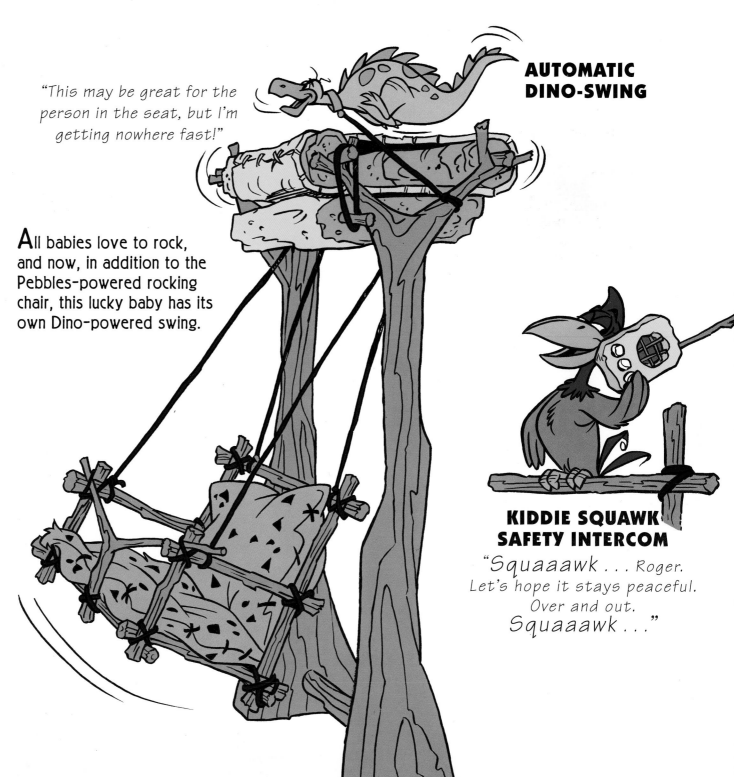

"This may be great for the person in the seat, but I'm getting nowhere fast!"

All babies love to rock, and now, in addition to the Pebbles-powered rocking chair, this lucky baby has its own Dino-powered swing.

KIDDIE SQUAWK SAFETY INTERCOM

"Squaaaawk . . . Roger. Let's hope it stays peaceful. Over and out. Squaaaawk . . ."

PLUG IT IN, TURN IT ON, AND WATCH WHAT HAPPENS!

1.

2.

3.

Look how easy it is to electrify these super-modern conveniences. Simply insert the cable plug into the eel's mouth and it sends a surge of electricity through the lines to light up, turn on, and charge every live-action appliance in the house.

4.

"Whewwww! This may light up their life, but it sure takes the fizzle out of me!"

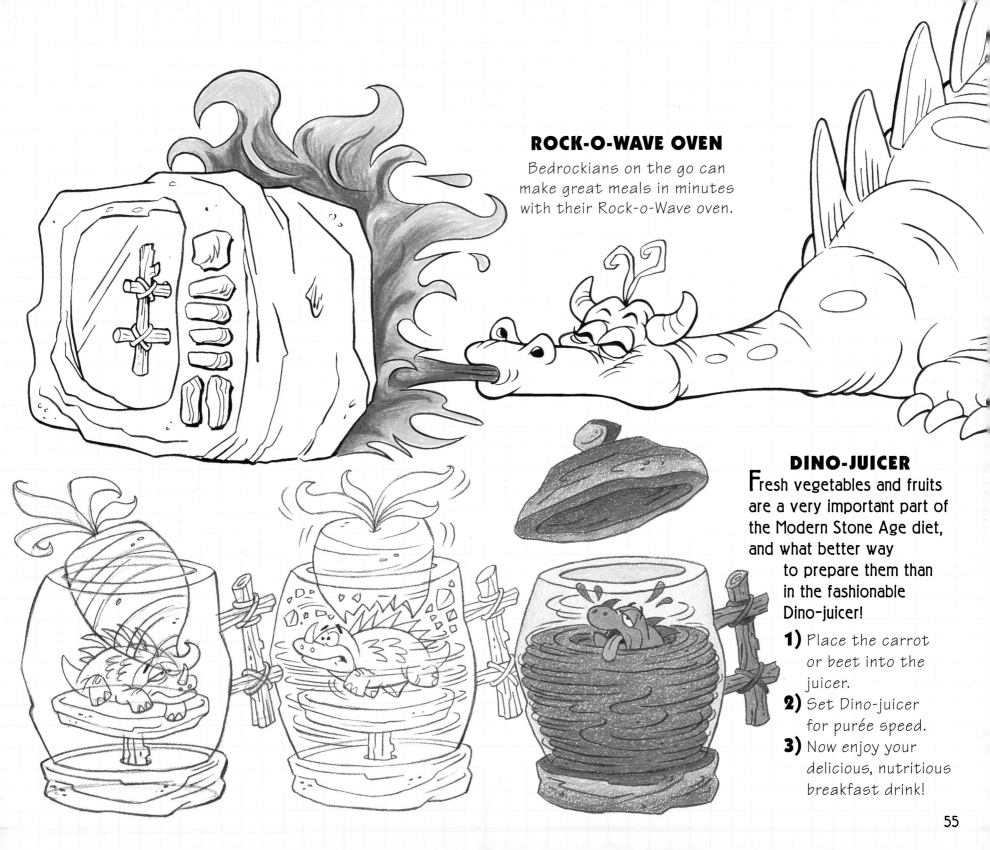

ROCK-O-WAVE OVEN

Bedrockians on the go can make great meals in minutes with their Rock-o-Wave oven.

DINO-JUICER

Fresh vegetables and fruits are a very important part of the Modern Stone Age diet, and what better way to prepare them than in the fashionable Dino-juicer!

1) Place the carrot or beet into the juicer.

2) Set Dino-juicer for purée speed.

3) Now enjoy your delicious, nutritious breakfast drink!

GET THE PICTURE?

Cable TV and satellite dishes have turned the Stone Age into the information age by bringing events around the globe into every Bedrock living room.

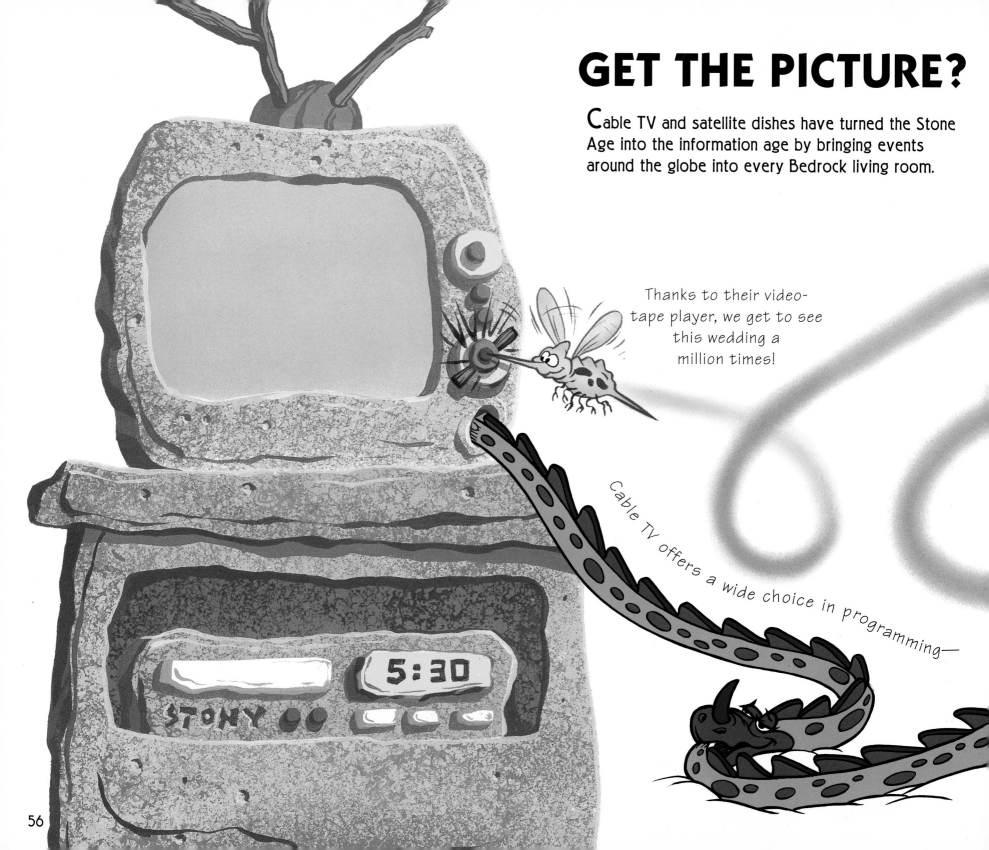

Thanks to their video-tape player, we get to see this wedding a million times!

Cable TV offers a wide choice in programming—

TORTOISE-SATELLITE-DISH

Some folks object to the huge Tortoise-satellite-dish atop their neighbors' roofs, but progress marches on, and this technology is clearly the wave of the future.

EEL CABLES

Nearly every home is cable ready. Bedrockians just give their local cable company a call and someone comes out to hook up as many Eel cables as needed for a perfect picture and loads of channels.

"Lying around up here is the best job I've *ever* had!"

as long as these guys keep their grips!

Whether it's hard rock, classic rock, or country rock, everyone's music sounds great on the latest stereo system. Here is a fabulous, compact stereo radio that Pebbles listens to at the office. It's got great sound and it's small enough to fit on almost any shelf.

Experts say the real listening pleasure is all in the speakers. To get the strongest and cleanest bass notes possible, the "woofer" in the speaker must be large enough. For bright, clear, high sounds, the "tweeters" must be fine-tuned and sharp.

SQUAWKIN' HEADPHONES

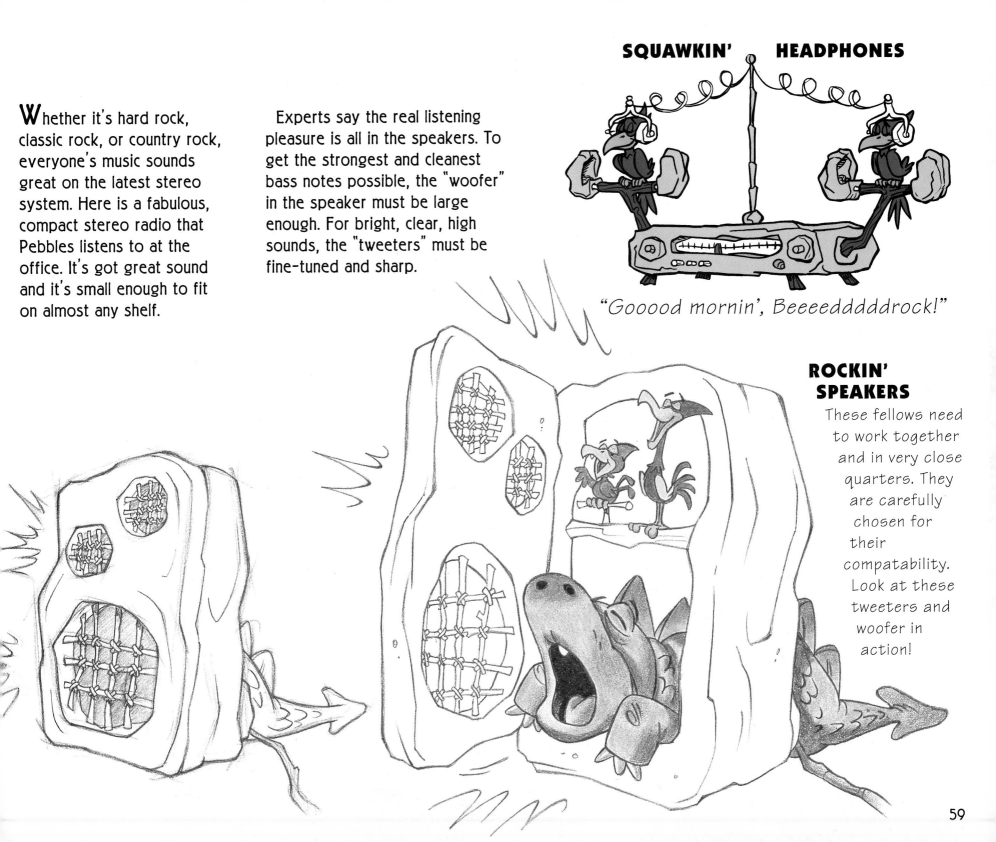

"Gooood mornin', Beeeedddddrock!"

ROCKIN' SPEAKERS

These fellows need to work together and in very close quarters. They are carefully chosen for their compatability. Look at these tweeters and woofer in action!

JAMMIN'!

Traffic in Bedrock is no better than in any other big city. Even the latest, most modern traffic lights get worn to a frazzle when so many cars, trucks, and buses want to go in different directions all at the same time.

"I sure wish we could find a short cut around that Brontobus," Fred groans. "Yeah, it's too bad we can't transform this jalopy into a Twirly Birdcopter," Barney chimes in. "We'd be bowling already!"

STOP AND GO...

Getting around town used to be a nightmare, but with Modern Stone Age traffic control, things flow smoothly. Every intersection has a stop sign, or stoplight, letting drivers know exactly who has the right of way. This Monkey signal has to be relieved regularly because its arms get tired.

"This job is tough enough without all the honking every time I make them stop."

MONKEY SIGNAL

Monkey signals are reliable as long as they don't work too many rush hours in a row.

TRAFFIC!

"Never mind feeding the meter. I could use a little snack myself!"

DOUBLE-BEAVER SIGNAL

BIRD-STOPLIGHT

BIRD-O-METER

HOURGLASS PARKING METER

The Double-Beaver signal, when properly fed, is very easy to see and is almost problem-free. One of the earliest signals was the Bird-stoplight. They proved unreliable because their candles did not stay lit long enough, so most of these old birds were eventually exchanged for the newer Double-Beavers.

63

THE BRONTO-BRIDGE

"I could sure use a neck-and-tail massage about now."

For years, crossing Bedrock River was almost impossible. Now the Bronto-bridge makes getting to the other side easy. The bridge opens to let tall ships and boats through, but it can snap down for traffic in an instant! Heads up, tails down!

Clear the way!
The Fire Mammoth is headed to an emergency.

BIRD SIREN

Bedrock's finest have what it takes to get the attention of any speeding motorist!

"Hit that siren!"

MODERN STONE AGE CLASSICS

'63 THERAPSIDA COUP

'58 GEOSAURUS

'57 BUGASAURUS

'70 CARIAMA

'81 THEROPED 100

'82 ALLOSAURUS

'83 RAPTOROADSTER

'84 DIATRYMA

'87 SCOLOSAURUS

'89 ULTRASAURUS COUP

'88 TRICER

'68 LOGROVER

'62 STEGO

'93 CANOPYSAURUS

'31 PACKASAURUS

'90 ANATOSAURUS

ON THE ROAD AGAIN

From dragsters and economy compacts to the classic family sedan, Bedrock's auto industry is booming. And maintenance is easy—even Betty can change a broken rock-wheel on her sporty little soft-top. It's as easy as 1, 2, 3. Just see for yourself!

LICENSE

Betty Rubble

Each day Betty and Wilma wait to hear the familiar *"pat, pat, pat"* of Fred and Barney's feet as they drive home from the quarry.

"Glad that's his head and not mine."

'91 SUPERSAURUS

UP, UP, AND AWAYYYY...

Flying from Bedrock to Rock Vegas or Hollyrock is a breeze, but taking off can be a bit jarring. The big planes are shot into the sky by a giant slingshot.

Once aloft the bird engines kick in and they fly a smooth and steady course (see Figure A). Finally, the Landing-gear birds descend, putting on the brakes for a gentle touch-down. If your luggage doesn't get lost, air travel is the only way to go!

Loading this many bags each day, it's no wonder the Stegosaurus baggage truck sometimes puts them onto the wrong plane.

Figure A

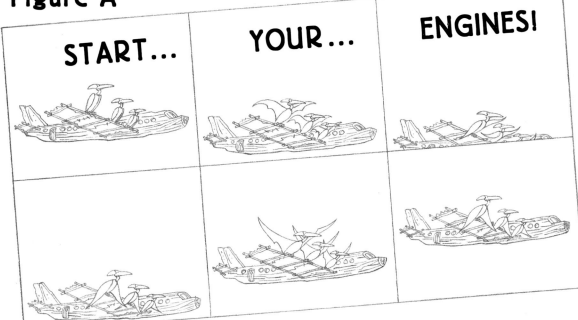

START... YOUR... ENGINES!

"Keep pedaling!"

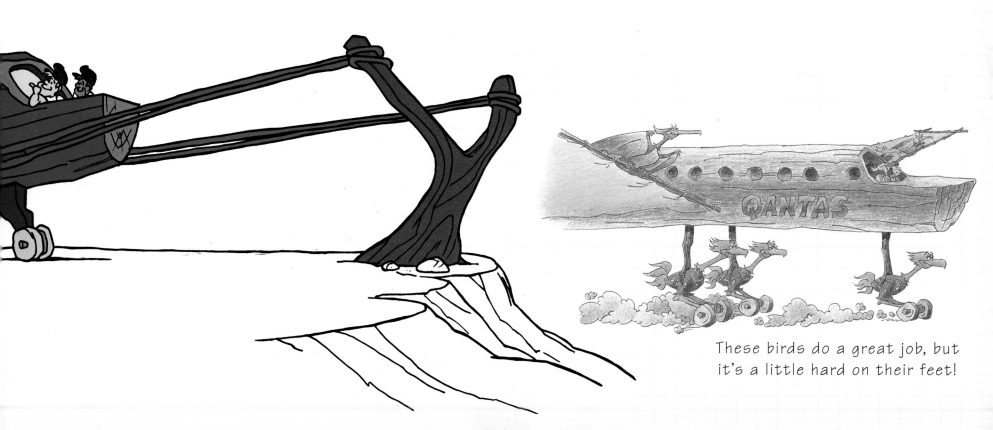

These birds do a great job, but it's a little hard on their feet!

DRAGON-ENGINE SPECIAL

At rest, the Dragon-Engine Special is a very impressive sight. But at top speed, roaring down the tracks, it's truly a Modern Stone Age wonder!

DOUBLE-BIRD HANDCAR

The Double-Bird handcar helps railroad workers check out the track for miles and miles.

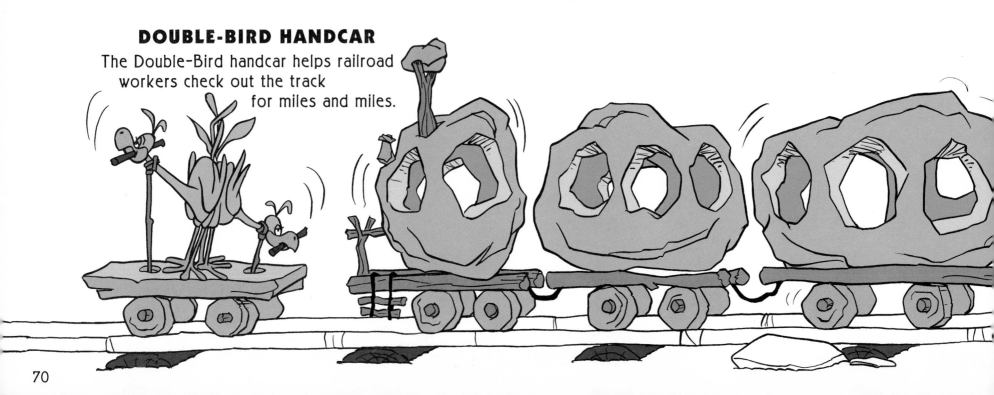

Every few hours, this beast has to stop and stoke its fire.

ALL ABOARD THE DRAGON-TRAIN!

For those folks who can take a little more time and enjoy the scenery, Bedrock's Dragon-Engine Special is just the ticket. Monkey crossing bars protect the train and the traffic from getting in each other's way, but when the Dragon-Engine Special gets a full head of steam, it's not easy to slow him down!

RR X XING

BOWL-A-RAMA

Bowling may be Fred's favorite sport, but nobody said he rolled a strike every time. "That's right, Fred," says Wilma between belly laughs, "throw yourself into it!"

A YABBA-DABBA-DOO GOOD TIME

Right in the heart of Bedrock is Fred Flintstone's favorite place, the fully automated Bedrock Bowl-a-Rama! Here, Fred can get his fill of bowling and fill up on his favorite snacks, too. Fresh Drago-Popper popcorn is one of his favorites.

Making perfect popcorn calls for nimble fingers and a mini-dragon who likes to be tickled. The popcorn vendor simply finds the mini-dragon's ticklish spot, and her fiery giggle does the rest.

DRAGO-POPPER

POPCORN

PINSETTERS

Even setting the pins is streamlined at the Bedrock Bowl-a-Rama. What used to be handled (or "tailed"), by the monkey-setter, is now the job of the giant Bronto-Bowl-a-Rama. This huge dino is able to scoop up fallen pins, organize them between his teeth, and neatly set them up all in a matter of seconds—**what a mouthful!**

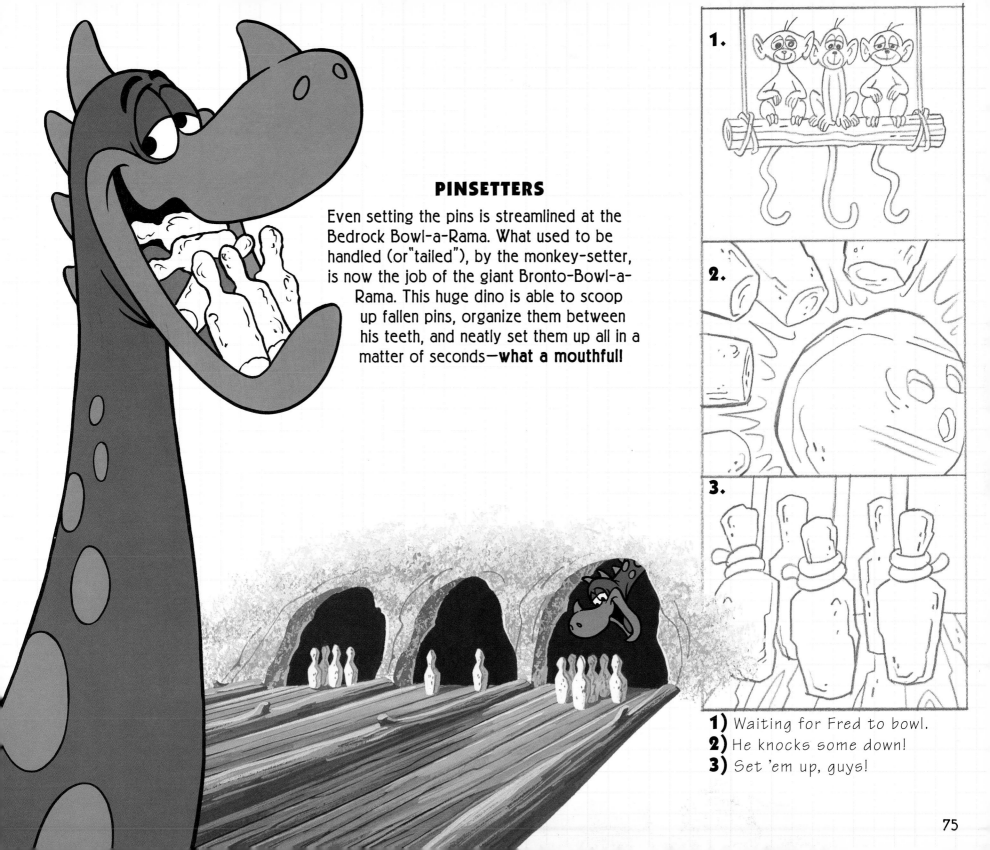

1.

2.

3.

1) Waiting for Fred to bowl.
2) He knocks some down!
3) Set 'em up, guys!

PINBALL WIZARDS AND VIDEO KIDS

While the older folks are bowling up a storm, the kids can usually be found pressing buttons and flipping switches at the pinball and video arcade at the Bedrock Bowl-a-Rama.

The object of Super Buzzio Brothers is to "zap" as many flying bees as possible in 60 seconds. Although the game does not hurt the little guys, it certainly shakes them up. That's why each arcade has a First-Aid bee, to carry off any of the Buzzio Brothers in need of a rest!

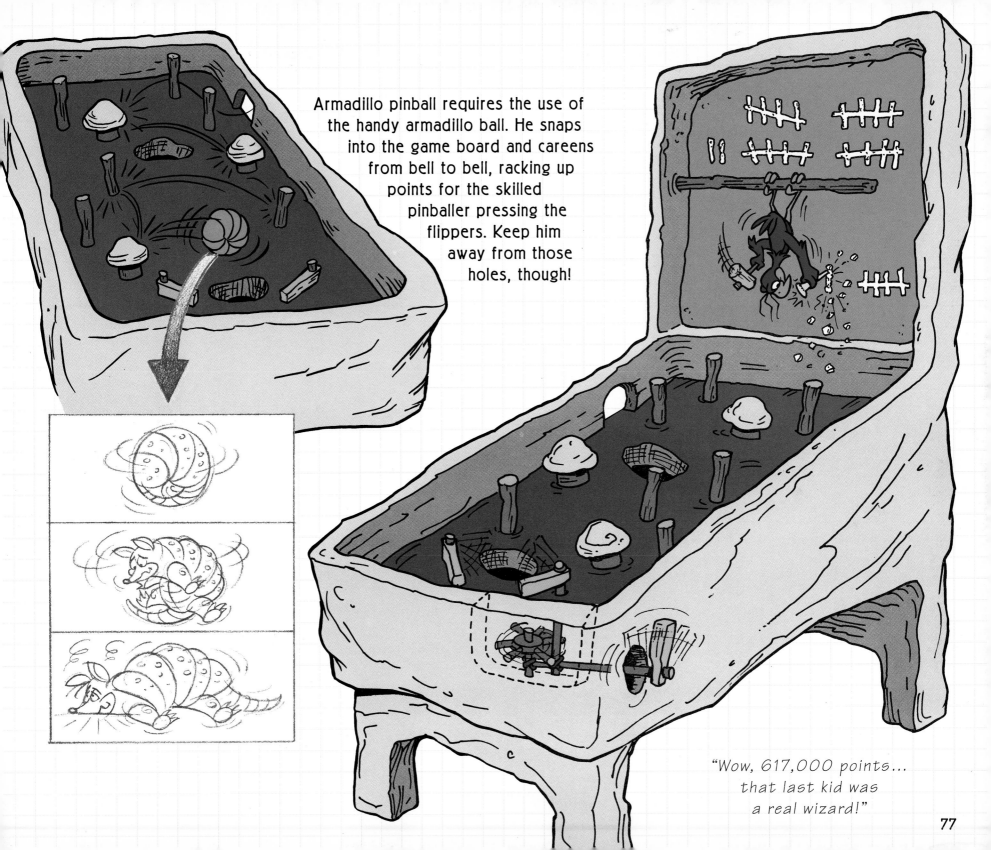

Armadillo pinball requires the use of the handy armadillo ball. He snaps into the game board and careens from bell to bell, racking up points for the skilled pinballer pressing the flippers. Keep him away from those holes, though!

"Wow, 617,000 points... that last kid was a real wizard!"

77

GOODNIGHT, BEDROCK

Home again at the end of another Modern Stone Age day. Fred and Wilma say goodnight to Barney and Betty. It's been another long and busy day, but, thanks to Bedrock Power and Light, the city is still aglow.

"Don't forget to put the cat out, Fred," Wilma calls sleepily from inside the house.

"Yabba-Dabba-Doo!"

When Fred and Wilma made their first television appearance all those years ago, the face of cartoons was changed forever. Dressed in stylish saber-tooth skins and as modern as they could be, the Flintstones characters captured a unique style of humor that made them a favorite with young and old alike.

The look of the characters and of the place, the hilarious slap-stick adventures, the multitude of memorable moments, and, of course, those wonderful wacky inventions, are all products of some amazingly talented folks. This book is dedicated to the creative genius of Bill Hanna and Joe Barbera and to the many artists who developed and perfected The Flintstones over the years. Without the vision and ability of these gifted people, this book and the decades of Modern Stone Age fun that inspired it would never have been.

Thanks for the laughs, fellows!